INTRODUCTION

The rugged interior and isolated waterways of Fiordland have attracted the adventurer for centuries. History records southern Maori battling the stormy waters of Foveaux Strait in unua (double-hulled canoes), European explorers in sailing ships, whalers and sealers arriving from across the Tasman Sea, all following the legends and charts of those before extolling the magnificence of this remote south-west corner of New Zealand. It is a unique area with an equally unique history of early Maori and European exploration of terrain that, from the air, appears impenetrable.

Fiordland National Park, part of the Te Wahipounamu/ South West New Zealand World Heritage Area, is unequalled in mountain grandeur, dense alpine forest, tranquil lakes and fiord-indented coastline. The park consists of designated 'Special Areas' to protect endangered species and vegetation; wilderness areas with foot access only; natural environment areas where bridges, huts and tracks are provided; and facilities areas for visitors' use, but with minimal disturbance to flora and fauna.

Through the feats of adventurers of the past Fiordland offers to those of the present the same enticement—high mountains to conquer, forest and alpine passes to tramp, lakes and fiords to kayak and sail, and rivers to fish, as well as a road leading through some of the most amazing landscape in the world.

TE ANAU

Te Anau in Western Southland is the gateway to Fiordland. The township is built sympathetically around the foreshore of Lake Te Anau, the largest of the South Island lakes, and it is from here that visitors to Fiordland National Park set out for an experience of a lifetime. The Department of Conservation Headquarters is situated on the lake edge and buses, helicopters, floatplanes and launches are available to transport tourists and outdoor pursuit enthusiasts to the remote corners of this the largest of the New Zealand National Parks. Lake Te Anau, serenely framed by snow-capped peaks of the Kepler Mountains *(above & opposite)* is just the beginning.

EGLINTON VALLEY

The road to Milford Sound is world famous—an amazing journey. After leaving the shoreline of Lake Te Anau it follows the gently flowing Eglinton River *(above & top right)*. Sheep and cattle graze peacefully beside clear mountain stream and superb alpine scenery. Suddenly the road disappears dramatically into tall beech forest and passes the seemingly ever present reflections of the Mirror Lakes *(top left)*. Lake Gunn *(opposite)* is an excellent trout fishing lake, one of several small lakes discovered by George Gunn and David McKellar in 1861 while searching for grazing pasture for their stock. Having set off from Lake Wakatipu these two sheep farmers, cum explorers, were the first Europeans to sight the Fiordland seacoast from Key Summit, deep in the mountainous interior.

HOLLYFORD VALLEY

The Hollyford Valley section of the road climbs steadily and follows the Upper Hollyford River *(top right)* through dense mountainous forest, passing numerous side streams and waterfalls such as Falls Creek *(top left)*. It emerges on bushline clearings to give sensational views of towering rock faces incredibly still supporting lush vegetation, cascading with waterfalls or glittering with stalactites of ice and pockets of snow. Above the bushline the vista widens to the grandeur of granite peaks, like Mounts Crosscut *(top centre)* and Talbot 2225 m *(opposite)* as the road approaches the Homer Tunnel *(above)*. The New Zealand Alpine Club Hut here offers a base for some of the best rock climbs in New Zealand.

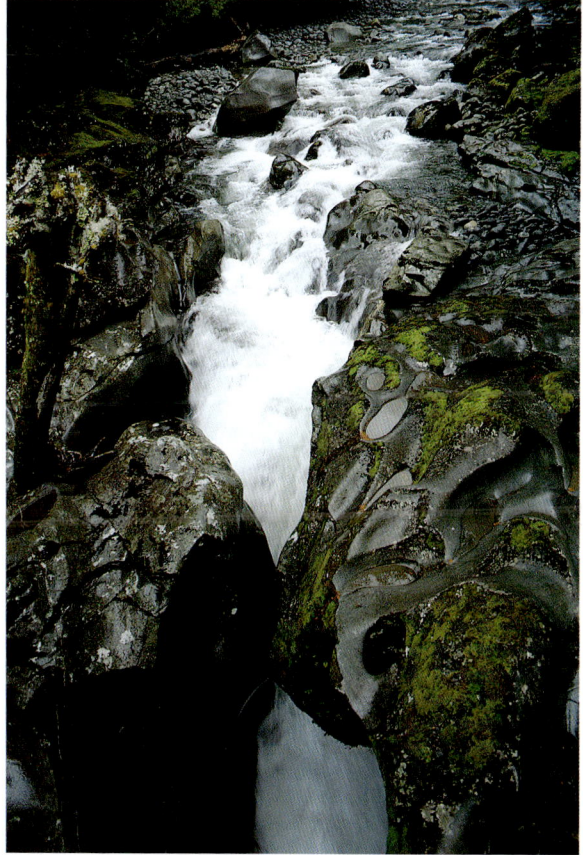

CLEDDAU VALLEY

When emerging from the dark, rough rock hewn walls at the western portal of the Homer Tunnel at the head of the Cleddau Valley, one feels the full impact of what an amazing feat of early engineering this tunnel is. It was first conceived by W. H. Homer in 1889. Road access from Te Anau was begun in 1929 by more than two hundred unemployed men during the New Zealand Depression, armed solely with shovels and wheelbarrows. Work on the piercing of the 1200 metre long, 1 in 10 gradient tunnel began in 1940. Atrocious working and weather conditions, avalanche damage, loss of lives and finally war delayed completion until 1953. From the western portal the road drops dramatically into the depths of the Cleddau Valley *(opposite)*. At the Chasm *(above right)* the Cleddau River falls almost vertically before continuing its run toward Milford Sound *(above left)*.

MILFORD SOUND

The road from Te Anau to Milford Sound has made accessible to all some of New Zealand's greatest scenery. It climaxes with the classical view of Milford Sound with Mitre Peak rising 1692 m skyward *(opposite above)*. Sheer cliffs soar vertically from the depths of the fiord's seabed *(top right)* and because of the high annual rainfall of 6236 mm, are often a multitude of waterfalls sourced from alpine lakes and hanging valleys high above. The Bowen Falls *(top left)* are within walking distance, but to fully appreciate the serenity and stillness of the Sound and soaring surrounding peaks such as the Lion 1302 m *(above)* a launch trip the 15 km length of the narrow canyon is recommended. The sight of the last rays of sun on Mitre Peak in Milford Sound *(opposite)* is the sight of a lifetime.

ROUTEBURN TRACK

The Routeburn Track through Mt Aspiring and Fiordland National Parks was discovered by gold prospector Patrick Quirk Caples in 1863. He trekked from Lake Wakatipu via the Routeburn, Greenstone and Hollyford Rivers out to Martins Bay in South Westland, becoming the first European to explore the luxuriantly forested Lower Hollyford Valley.

The Routeburn section, *(above)* 35km in all, traverses the Humboldt mountains via the Harris Saddle, linking the Dart and Hollyford valleys. Lake Mackenzie *(top above)* with Ocean Peak and Mount Emily at its head is on the Hollyford, thus Fiordland, side of the saddle, whereas the Routeburn Falls *(opposite)* leads down into Mt Aspiring National Park.

MILFORD TRACK

Quintin Mackinnon pioneered the opening to Milford Sound from the mountainous interior of Fiordland in 1888. Attempts had been made to find a pathway through the rugged alpine peaks *(top left above)* but it was Mackinnon and his companion Ernest Mitchell who succeeded in finding a niche in the near vertical precipices at the head of the Arthur Valley. From then until near his death Mackinnon continued to maintain the track and guide parties from Te Anau into Milford, acting as the local postman at the same time. Today the Milford Track is regarded as "the finest walk in the world". It begins with a leisurely launch trip to Glade House at the head of Lake Te Anau and a limbering walk through lush forest *(top right above)* the length of the Clinton River canyon *(opposite)* before the 1036 m climb over Mackinnon Pass and steep descent into the head of the Arthur Valley. A side track leads to the Sutherland Falls *(above),* New Zealand's highest with a drop of 580 m. The final day follows the Arthur River to Lake Ada where a launch waits to transport guided trampers back to the home comforts of the famous Milford Hotel.

The flora of Fiordland was enthusiastically described and illustrated by botanists on James Cook's voyages of discovery in the 1770s. Fiordland National Park is now part of the South West New Zealand World Heritage Area, giving further protection to its uniqueness and beauty for timeless enjoyment.

East of the Main Divide the forest vegetation is dominantly alpine beech, whereas podocarps appear on the wetter western slopes. The Lower Hollyford Valley is renowned for its glades of the silvery Prince of Wales Feathers fern which carpet the forest floor. The red flowering southern rata *(middle opposite)* is a cousin to the North Island pohutukawa.

Lake Marian *(above)* nestles above the bushline in the Lower Hollyford. A walking track to, and around this gem of the Fiordland lakes displays the full range of vegetation, from forest floor to sub-alpine scree. You may find a mountain daisy *(below opposite)* or Mt. Cook Lily *(top opposite)* among the higher alpine flora.

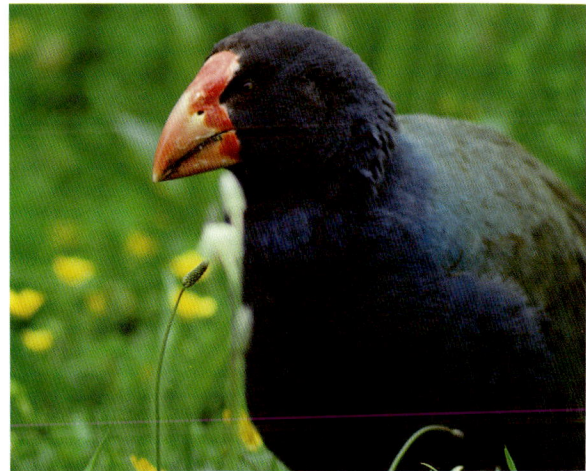

The geology of Fiordland is as diverse as it is spectacular. Rugged granite peaks, hanging valleys, alpine lakes, smooth walled cirques—all evidence of over two million years of glacial movement and erosion *(top above— Hauroko Saddle)*. In dramatic contrast are the heavily forested river valleys that lead to the many large lakes found within the park. The Grebe River *(opposite)* flows from high alpine country into the South Arm of Lake Manapouri.

The habitat of New Zealand's mountain parrot, the kea, *(left above)* is among the peaks where he has a reputation amongst climbers for his cheeky, often kleptomaniac habits. The flightless takahe *(right above)* was thought extinct until rediscovered amongst the snowtussock grassland beyond the western shores of Lake Te Anau by Dr G. B. Orbell, in 1948. A "Special Area" in the Murchison Mountains has been set aside for its protection, but survival is tenuous as only one chick is usually reared from the two or three eggs laid. A captive rearing programme in Te Anau is supported by the Department of Conservation and the Royal Forest and Bird Society.

GEORGE SOUND

George Sound, *(left above)* one of the most beautiful of the southern fiords, is reached by foot track from the northwest arm of the Middle Fiord of Lake Te Anau. It passes through primeval bush and mountain country to the head of the deep fiord, a route chosen by serious, rather than recreational trampers. These young adventurers are approaching the top of Henry Pass *(left below)* before dropping to the still waters of Lake Katherine *(above).* There is history to add to the appeal of isolation and unblemished landscape that George Sound offers. The last traces of tribal relics of early West Coast Maori, most likely driven deep into these mountains by warlike enemies, were discovered here. Also eighteen of the fabled Fiordland Wapiti were released at the head of the sound in 1905. They were, in part, a gift from the President of the United States of America, Theodore Roosevelt.

KEPLER TRACK

Lake Manapouri, *(middle & below opposite)* Maori legend says, was formed by the tears of two sisters, Moturau and Koronae. Its original name was Roto-ua "Rainy Lake" bestowed upon it by a ninth century high chief Rakaehautu. It became known as "Moturau" and the present name "Manapouri" is a misnomer made by an early surveyor charting the area. Tranquil Lake Manapouri with its thirty-odd bushclad islets is a major Fiordland attraction.

The Kepler Track was opened in 1988, linking Lakes Te Anau and Manapouri by way of the Waiau River outlet where it begins and ends. The track follows Lake Te Anau's western shoreline before climbing steadily up Mount Luxmore. Wonderful alpine and lake panoramas are to be had along the ridgeline *(top opposite)*. It descends again into verdant forest along the shores of Lake Manapouri *(above)* where magic glimpses are enjoyed from secluded sandy beaches. The 67 km of wide, well-graded track with excellent shelters and hut accommodation is a Fiordland experience for all.

DOUBTFUL SOUND

Described by Captain Cook in 1770 as "a very snug harbour", Doubtful Sound is an idyllic day excursion from Pearl Harbour, Lake Manapouri. A launch trip to West Arm, a 20 km bus ride up and over Wilmot Pass and you arrive at Peaceful Deep Cove, Doubtful Sound *(opposite)*. A second tourist launch takes you to Halls Arm, a quiet unspoiled waterway of Fiordland. After rain, a frequent occurrence in this south western corner of New Zealand, the sheer rock and bushclad walls of the sound are a veil of waterfalls *(top left above)* fed from alpine reservoirs such as Lake Bloxham *(top right above)*. Rainbows appear frequently against the rock of Commander Peak *(above)* which guards the entrance to Halls Arm. The heavy silence is broken only by the call of a bird or the sound of falling water. It's hard to associate this peace with the public outcry that arose in 1970 as a result of a proposed Hydro Scheme for Lake Manapouri which required the raising of the lake some 12 m. The compromise solution was an ingenious underground powerhouse 213 m below lake level at West Arm, with a 10 km tailrace tunnel bored through the mountains to Deep Cove.

DUSKY SOUND

On Captain Cook's first voyage to New Zealand in 1770 he sailed up Fiordland's coastline naming, but not entering Dusky Sound *(top above & over page)*. He noted "there must be shelter from all winds provided there be sufficient depth of water." He chose Dusky as an anchorage while repairing *The Resolution* and resting his crew after an arduous 123 days at sea on his return voyage in 1773. After $6\frac{1}{2}$ weeks he recorded "there is no port in New Zealand I have been in that affords the necessary refreshments in such plenty as Dusky Bay." It was on Indian Island *(opposite)* that Cook first made contact with the New Zealand Maori, a family of the Ngati-Mamoe tribe. Detailed observations were recorded and have been a valuable account of traditional Maori life in 18th century Fiordland. Dusky Sound is dominated to the north by Resolution Island, *(above)* the scene of New Zealand's first recorded shipwreck. *The Endeavour*, already declared unseaworthy after leaving Sydney on a passenger voyage to India, finally broke up on rocks off Facile Harbour. Along with crew and passengers and 48 stowaways found onboard, the total of castaways in Dusky Sound at that time in 1795 numbered 244!

Dusky Sound is the largest fiord in New Zealand and place names within the passages and coves of the 43.9 km sound tell much of the area. On his first voyage Cook approached at "dusk" which influenced his decision not to enter. Resolution Island is named after the sailing ship of his second voyage and Nine Fathom Passage *(top left above)* confirms his belief in a deep anchorage. Parrot, Pigeon, Petrel and Shag Islands, Crayfish and Porpoise Points and Seal Islands refer to the abundant bird and marine life present. Indian Island was how Cook referred to the native peoples he met there and Supper Cove and Canoe Harbour, Indian Island *(top right above)* are self-explanatory. The southern Maori discovered here travelled by double-hulled sea canoe from villages around Foveaux Strait. They stayed for months at a time because of the ready source of food. A rock stack on Chalky Island *(opposite)* marks the entrance to Chalky Inlet *(above)* named by early sealers. Ancient Maori sleeping platforms, fireplaces and midden (shellfood remains) are found in many rock shelters and caves within Dusky Sound.